D0908571

GRAPHIC LIBRARY™

INVENTIONS AND DISCOVERY

MADAM C. J. WALKER AND
NEW COSMETICS

by Katherine Krohn

illustrated by Richard Dominguez, Dave Hoover,
Bill Anderson, and Charles Barnett III

Consultant:
A'Lelia Bundles
Great-great-granddaughter of Madam C. J. Walker
Author, *On Her Own Ground: The Life and Times of
Madam C. J. Walker*

Capstone
press

Mankato, Minnesota

Graphic Library is published by Capstone Press,
151 Good Counsel Drive, P.O. Box 669, Mankato, Minnesota 56002.
www.capstonepress.com

1 2 3 4 5 6 11 10 09 08 07 06

Library of Congress Cataloging-in-Publication Data
Krohn, Katherine E.
    Madam C. J. Walker and new cosmetics / by Katherine Krohn; illustrated by Richard
Dominguez . . . [et al.].
        p. cm.—(Graphic library. Inventions and discovery)
    Includes bibliographical references and index.
    ISBN-13: 978-0-7368-6485-5 (hardcover)
    ISBN-10: 0-7368-6485-7 (hardcover)
    ISBN-13: 978-0-7368-7520-2 (softcover pbk.)
    ISBN-10: 0-7368-7520-4 (softcover pbk.)
    1. Walker, C. J., Madam, 1867–1919—Juvenile literature. 2. African American women
executives—Biography—Juvenile literature. 3. Cosmetics industry—United States—History—
Juvenile literature. 4. Women millionaires—United States—Biography—Juvenile literature.
I. Dominguez, Richard. II. Title. III. Series.
HD9970.5.C672K76 2007
338.7'66855092—dc22   2006004080

Summary: In graphic novel format, tells the story of Madam C. J. Walker, who invented a line of
    African American hair products and cosmetics that helped her become the first self-made female
    millionaire of any race.

Designer
Alison Thiele

Colorist
Benjamin Hunzeker

Editor
Christine Peterson

Editor's note: Direct quotations from primary sources are indicated by a yellow background.

Direct quotations appear on the following pages:
Page 21, from Madam C. J. Walker's speech before the 1912 convention of the National Negro
    Business League, as recorded by the NNBL; page 23, from a 1913 speech by Madam C. J.
    Walker; as published in *On Her Own Ground: The Life and Times of Madam C. J. Walker*,
    by A'Lelia Bundles (New York: Scribner, 2001).

TABLE OF CONTENTS

Annie hired Sarah to sell her products door-to-door and give scalp treatments. Sarah now made more money than she did washing clothes.

Do you think this treatment will help my hair?

Yes, I do, ma'am. My hair used to be in worse shape than yours.

The trick is to wash your hair often and use this shampoo.

And you're sure that will help?

Hair cannot grow unless the scalp is clean and healthy.

Sarah also found time to take classes at a night school in St. Louis. Sarah studied geography, reading, and bookkeeping.

I must improve my mind if I'm going to improve my life.

By 1905, Sarah was a successful sales agent for Pope-Turnbo. But she wanted more. That year, Sarah moved to Denver, Colorado, to be near family. There she worked in the kitchen of a boardinghouse.

I'm sure I can sell products to women at the boardinghouse. The extra money will help.

I hear you sell hair products.

That's right.

My hair is so dry. Nothing seems to help.

It's no wonder with all the salt in the water. But I have something that will help.

Yes, but this one really works.

Really? I've tried lots of different products.

When Sarah had all of the ingredients from her dream, she began to experiment in her kitchen.

This doesn't seem quite the right thickness. I'll add another cup of petrolatum.

A little more sulfur . . .

Ooohh that stinks. Needs more violet extract.

I've finally got the right formula, Charles. I think it's ready to sell.

You look wonderful, Sarah. Your hair grower really works.

In 1906, Sarah married Charles Joseph "C. J." Walker. She changed her name to Madam C. J. Walker.

11

Surely you are not going to shut the door in my face. I feel that I am in a business that is a credit to the womanhood of our race.

They did not believe such a thing could be done, but I have proven beyond question of a doubt that I do grow hair.

Everybody told me that I was making a mistake by going into this business, but I know how to grow hair as well as I know how to grow cotton.

Madam's speech moved Booker T. Washington. She showed him her power and determination as a business leader. The next year, he invited Walker to speak at the NNBL convention.

NNBL

21

Madam Walker moved to New York City in 1916. She opened a new Lelia College and salon in the first floor of a house she bought in Harlem.

Women, what paves the way to business success?

Good grooming?

Absolutely. That and hard work.

I never thought I could run my own business, until I took Madam's course.

Did you know she used to be a washerwoman, just like us?

Madam Walker's products helped many African American women improve the health of their hair. Her popular line of cosmetics made her the first self-made female millionaire of any race in the United States.

I say to every woman in this room, don't sit down and wait for the opportunities to come.

Get up and make them happen!

Madam C. J. Walker is remembered for her creativity and ambition as an inventor. She remains an inspiring, encouraging voice for African American women.

More about

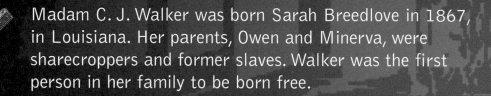

Madam C. J. Walker

Madam C. J. Walker was born Sarah Breedlove in 1867, in Louisiana. Her parents, Owen and Minerva, were sharecroppers and former slaves. Walker was the first person in her family to be born free.

Madam Walker was orphaned at age 6, married at 14, and had her only child, Lelia, at 17. Madam Walker was a widow by age 20.

After she invented Wonderful Hair Grower, Madam Walker put together the packaging for her product. She bought tins from the American Can Company. A man from her church, who owned a printing press, printed labels for the tins.

Some people falsely believe that Madam Walker invented the hair straightening comb. However, she did use a wide-toothed steel comb, heated on a stove, with Glossine. This method made hair look longer and straighter.

Madam Walker created the Madam Walker Beauty Culturists Union. Each member paid yearly dues. The money helped employees in times of need.

Madam Walker died on May 25, 1919. Her last words were, "I want to live to help my race."

After her mother's death, Lelia ran the cosmetics company. Lelia died in 1931. The company remained in the Walker family until 1985 when the business was sold.

Today, Madam Walker's Indianapolis factory is a National Historic Landmark. The building houses the Madam Walker Theater Center, a center for African American art and culture. Madam Walker's mansion, Villa Lewaro, is also a National Historic Landmark. The home is a private residence.

In 1998, the United States Post Office released a postage stamp honoring Madam C. J. Walker.

GLOSSARY

agent (AY-juhnt)—someone who arranges or sells things for other people

demonstrate (DEM-uhn-strate)—to show other people how to do something or use something

scalp treatment (SKALP TREET-muhnt)—the process of applying products to the head to help heal sores

sulfur (SUHL-fur)—a yellow chemical sometimes used to treat skin diseases

tetter (TET-tur)—a skin disease, often of the scalp, that causes sores and itching

tonic (TON-ik)—a liquid sometimes used to heal skin diseases

INTERNET SITES

FactHound offers a safe, fun way to find Internet sites related to this book. All of the sites on FactHound have been researched by our staff.

Here's how:
1. Visit *www.facthound.com*
2. Choose your grade level.
3. Type in this book ID **0736864857** for age-appropriate sites. You may also browse subjects by clicking on letters, or by clicking on pictures and words.
4. Click on the **Fetch It** button.

FactHound will fetch the best sites for you!

READ MORE

Hall, Margaret. *Madam C. J. Walker.* Lives and Times. Chicago: Heinemann, 2003.

Hobkirk, Lori. *Madam C. J. Walker.* Journey to Freedom. Chanhassen, Minn.: Child's World, 2001.

McKissack, Patricia, and Fredrick McKissak. *Madam C. J. Walker: Self-Made Millionaire.* Great African Americans. Berkeley Heights, N.J.: Enslow, 2001.

Nichols, Catherine. *Madam C. J. Walker.* Scholastic News Nonfiction Readers. New York: Children's Press, 2005.

Sullivan, Otha Richard. *African American Women Scientists and Inventors.* Black Stars. New York: Wiley, 2002.

BIBLIOGRAPHY

Bundles, A'Lelia. *On Her Own Ground: The Life and Times of Madam C. J. Walker.* New York: Scribner, 2001.

Madam C. J. Walker Papers. Indiana Historical Society, Indianapolis, Ind. (http://www.indianahistory.org/library/manuscripts/collection_guides/m0399.html)

INDEX